CLOUDS AND CLOCKS

A Story For Children Who Soil

By Matthew Galvin, M.D.

Illustrated by Sandra Ferraro

MAGINATION PRESS

NEW YORK

Acknowledgements

The author and illustrator are grateful for the review of this book and the suggestions provided by Patricia Becker, M.D., Clinical Assistant Professor in the Department of Pediatrics, Indiana University School of Medicine, to Susan Kent Cakars and her associates at Magination Press for their patient editing, and to Dottie Maguire for her preparation of the manuscript.

Library of Congress Cataloging-in-Publication Data

Galvin, Matthew.
    Clouds and clocks : a story for children who soil / written by
Matthew R. Galvin ; illustrated by Sandra Ferraro.
        p.   cm.
    Summary: Upset and afraid when his beloved grandfather has to go
to the hospital, Andrew, whose working mother has little time for
him, develops a problem of his own when he stops using the toilet.
    ISBN 0-945354-15-0
    1. Encopresis in children—Juvenile literature.   [1. Soiling.]
I. Ferraro, Sandra, ill.   II. Title.
RJ456.E48G35   1989
618.92'849—dc20   89-12278
                                                                           CIP
                                                                           AC

Copyright © 1989 by Matthew R. Galvin
Published by
Magination Press
An Imprint of Brunner/Mazel, Inc., 19 Union Square West, New York, NY 10003
Paperback edition distributed to the trade by
Publishers Group West
4065 Hollis St., Emeryville, CA 94608
Telephone 800-365-3453; in CA call collect 415-658-3453
Distributed in Canada by
Book Center
1140 Beaulac St., Montreal, Quebec H4R 1R8, Canada

MANUFACTURED IN THE UNITED STATES OF AMERICA

10 9 8 7 6 5 4 3 2 1

FOREWORD TO PARENTS

Soiling (or encopresis) in preschool and school-age children is not uncommon. Estimates of prevalence among children of different ages vary. The American Psychiatric Association has estimated that approximately one percent of five-year-olds may have a problem with more than occasional soiling for periods longer than six months.* On the other hand, soiling is not commonly written about in articles and books for the parents and certainly not in stories for children. As a result, the child who soils and his (boys are affected more often than girls) family are left feeling isolated, frustrated and embarrassed. The purpose of this book is to reduce isolation, frustration and embarrassment so that families will seek help. The help that is needed will vary from child to child and from family to family. Sometimes the problem has a physical cause which a pediatrician or family doctor can identify and treat. Sometimes the problem has an emotional or behavioral cause instead. Even when the problem is rooted in such things as learning to use the toilet properly or getting used to toilets outside the home, there can be physical changes in the bowel that require a doctor's attention. Not every child and his family will require all the help that Andrew in this story receives. But it is hoped that any child who soils will feel better in the knowledge he is not alone and that treatment is available.

*Reference: *Diagnostic and Statistical Manual, Third Edition-Revised.* American Psychiatric Association, Washington, DC, 1987.

Andrew liked spending time with his grandfather. The two of them often sat on the porch, relaxing and looking up at the sky. They played a game of finding just the right names for different kinds of clouds. "That's a chalk-dust sky," Grandad might say. "Chalk-dust clouds on a blue chalkboard."

They did lots of things together. While Grandad nailed new shingles on the roof, Andrew pretended he was fixing the roof of the tool shed. Grandad called down, "Andy, look over there. What would you call that?"

Andrew looked up at the thin streaks of clouds with blue sky between them. "Tiger stripes!" he said.

Clouds made them think of many different things. Andrew saw castles and dinosaurs and herds of buffalo. A sky of swirling gray and white reminded Grandad of an oyster shell. Sometimes they could see a treasure map of shifting continents and islands. One sky reminded Grandad of Queen Anne's lace. Andrew and his grandfather had seen the white blossoms when they took a walk in the country.

Andrew and his mother lived with Grandad. Andrew's father had left them when Andrew was still a baby. Once he had asked his mother why, but she didn't want to talk about it. So he asked his grandfather.

Grandad explained, "Your mom and dad just didn't get along very well." Then he added, "Your dad left you something to remember him by."

It was his dad's watch. Andrew was very proud to have it, but he didn't know how to tell time. Grandad said, "You'll learn someday soon."

Andrew's mother worked all day and went to school at night. Often Andrew was in bed before she came home. Other nights she spent all her time on schoolwork. Andrew was sad that his mother worked so much, but he liked being with his grandfather.

But Grandad started to seem different to Andrew. He sometimes forgot things. And he spent more time alone in his room. Andrew didn't know why, and he was scared.

Andrew worried about Grandad. He didn't want to go to school and leave Grandad all alone. But Andrew's mother said he couldn't stay home with Grandad. Every morning as he ate breakfast, she said, "Hurry up or you'll be late." Then she told him to use the bathroom.

"I don't have to," Andrew always said. But when they were in the car, he changed his mind. His mother often got mad. She said he dawdled and wasted time. But she got him to school on time.

One day after school, Andrew's mother said, "Grandad isn't feeling well. He is going to the hospital."

"Why?" asked Andrew, trying hard not to cry.

"So the doctors can find out what the problem is," said Grandad, giving him a hug. "I'll be back soon, Andy."

Then Andrew began having a problem of his own. It happened in school the next day. He didn't want to use the bathroom there. When he needed to use it, he didn't. After a while Andrew went to the bathroom in his pants.

One of the kids shouted, "Andrew pooped in his pants!" Others teased him and called him "stinky." Andrew's teacher called it an "accident" and took him to the bathroom. She helped him clean up and said, "Everyone has an accident now and then." She made Andrew promise to try to use the toilet in time.

Andrew tried to keep his promise, but his problem didn't get any better. Instead, it got worse. He didn't even use the bathroom at home when he should. His mother was mad at him a lot, especially when she found the underpants full of poop that he had hidden under his bed.

"Andrew, why are you doing this?" she asked.

Andrew didn't say anything. He didn't even want to think about it. But he didn't like having his mom mad at him.

Finally, Andrew and his mother went to see Dr. Henry. Mom told Dr. Henry about Andrew's problem. Andrew wanted to hide. When Dr. Henry said, "I know many boys your age who have the same problem," Andrew was really surprised.

Dr. Henry asked Andrew if he wanted to find a way to solve the problem. "Yes," Andrew almost whispered.

"First of all," said Dr. Henry, "I'll need to check your bottom, just like I check your ears and throat."

After that, Dr. Henry explained, "Andy, your problem is called soiling. I'll give you one kind of medicine to clean your insides, then a medicine called mineral oil to take at breakfast time and again at dinner. You also need to sit on the toilet for ten minutes after breakfast and ten minutes after dinner to let the medicine work."

"Do I have to go to the hospital?" Andrew wondered.

"No," said Dr. Henry, but I would like you and your mother to see another doctor—one who talks and listens to children. Her name is Dr. Rachel."

In Dr. Rachel's office there was a round table with paper and lots of crayons. Dr. Rachel asked Andrew, "Can you tell me about your problem?"

Andrew felt embarrassed. "It's called soiling," he said. Then he added, "It's fixed now."

Dr. Rachel said, "I'm glad about that."

"I don't want to talk about it any more," Andrew told her.

"Okay," said Dr. Rachel. "Let's draw some pictures instead."

Andrew liked to draw. He drew a picture of his family at home. In the sky above the house, Andrew drew a dark whirling cloud. Dr. Rachel said, "That tornado looks scary."

Andrew nodded. Then he pointed to the man in the picture. "This is my Grandad," he said, "but he isn't home right now."

"Oh?" said Dr. Rachel. "Where is he?"

Andrew looked down. "In the hospital," he said softly.

"Tell me about your Grandad," suggested Dr. Rachel.

"I miss him," Andrew said, crying a little.

Andrew told Dr. Rachel about the cloud game he played with Grandad. Then Dr. Rachel asked about Andrew's mother.

"She's very busy," Andrew said. He didn't feel like talking about her. "I have a watch," he told Dr. Rachel, "but I can't tell time."

"You'll learn one day soon, Andy," Dr. Rachel said with a smile. "You know, your body can tell time." Andrew was surprised. "Your body can tell you when it's time to use the bathroom," explained Dr. Rachel.

"You mean like a clock?" asked Andrew.

"Sort of," replied Dr. Rachel. "We'll talk more about it next time."

But the next time Andrew saw Dr. Rachel, he didn't want to talk about his body. He had been taking the medicine, but he was still having accidents. He wouldn't even look at her. "I hate school!" he said at last.

"What do you hate about it?" asked Dr. Rachel.

"All the kids tease me all the time," Andrew told her.

"Sometimes that happens when a person soils," she said. "But it won't go on forever—especially when you've solved the problem."

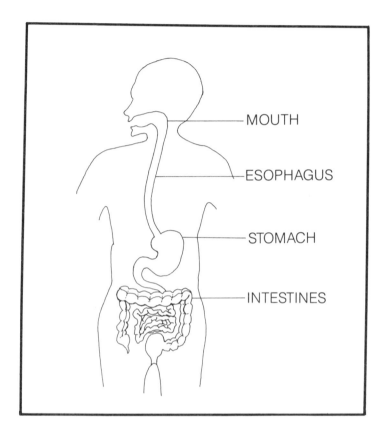

MOUTH

ESOPHAGUS

STOMACH

INTESTINES

Dr. Rachel showed Andrew a drawing. It showed how a person's stomach is connected to a long, curving tube called the intestine. "The tube is open at the bottom," she told him.

"Is that where the poop comes out?" asked Andrew.

"Right," said Dr. Rachel. "Your intestine is a special tube. It can tell when it's full of poop. It sends a message to your brain that it's time to use the toilet."

Andrew said, "But sometimes when I go to the bathroom nothing comes out, even when I push hard."

Dr. Rachel said, "When a person has stopped listening to his body for a while, sometimes the tube gets too full of poop. It stops sending messages to the brain."

Andrew thought for a minute. "Does that mean the clock in the body doesn't tell the right time any more?" he asked.

"It's not a real clock like your watch," said Dr. Rachel, "but that's the idea."

"How do you fix it?" asked Andrew.

Dr. Rachel said, "The mineral oil makes it work more smoothly. It lets the poop come out when you sit on the toilet. But you can help by relaxing."

"What's relaxing?" Andrew wanted to know.

"Relaxing," explained Dr. Rachel, "is when you let your body feel very good inside. You can use your imagination to help you." Dr. Rachel asked Andrew to remember a time when he felt very good inside.

Andrew thought about sitting on the porch with Grandad and playing the cloud game. He smiled. "I'm thinking about clouds," he told Dr. Rachel.

"Good," she said. "Now imagine a sky full of your favorite colors and beautiful clouds."

Andrew closed his eyes to imagine better. In his mind the clouds changed shape and drifted by. He wondered what they would become.

"You can drift with the clouds, feeling very good inside, if you like," he heard Dr. Rachel say.

When Andrew opened his eyes, he did feel very good inside. "There are all kinds of times you can use your imagination to relax," Dr. Rachel said.

"Like when I have to sit on the toilet after breakfast and dinner?" asked Andrew.

Dr. Rachel smiled. "If you like. It doesn't take a lot of time to relax." Then she said, "Now, let's ask your mother to come in. We'll tell her what we've been doing."

During the next few weeks, some good things began to happen. Andrew learned to relax. Andrew's mother told him that he was doing a good job using the bathroom on time after breakfast and after dinner. Sometimes she forgot the mineral oil and he reminded her. After a while he began to think that she needed to learn to relax, too. Andrew told her about using her imagination. He and his mom both began to spend time relaxing. Pretty soon he stopped soiling.

Andrew and his mother visited Dr. Rachel some more, even after the soiling stopped. They talked about different ways they could let each other know how they were feeling.

The kids at school didn't tease Andrew much any more. He made some new friends. One friend's father studied the weather. He came to school to talk about it. Andrew was excited, especially when they learned about clouds. School was a good place to learn about all kinds of things. Andrew even began to learn how to tell time.

The very best thing that happened, though, was that Grandad came home from the hospital. He told Andrew that he had to take some medicine, too.

"Are you feeling better now?" Andrew asked.

Grandad said, "Yes, I am. The medicine and talking to the doctor help."

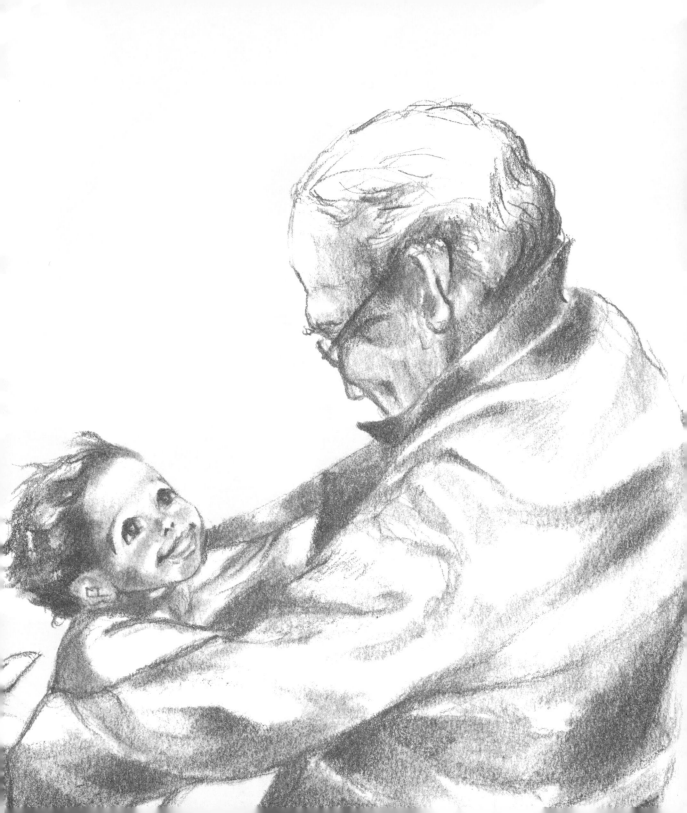

After that, they went for a walk together.

Other Magination Press Books include:

Cartoon Magic: How to Help Children Discover Their Rainbows Within
by Richard J. Crowley, Ph.D., and Joyce C. Mills, Ph.D.
Clouds and Clocks: A Story for Children Who Soil
by Matthew Galvin, M.D.
*Gran-Gran's Best Trick: A Story for Children Who Have Lost
Someone They Love*
by L. Dwight Holden, M.D.
Ignatius Finds Help: A Story About Psychotherapy for Children
by Matthew Galvin, M.D.
Lizard Tales: Observations About Life
by William R. Davis, M.D.
*Otto Learns About His Medicine: A Story About Medication for
Hyperactive Children*
by Matthew Galvin, M.D.
Robby Really Transforms: A Story About Grown-ups Helping Children
by Matthew Galvin, M.D.
*Sammy the Elephant and Mr. Camel: A Story to Help Children
Overcome Bedwetting While Discovering Self-Appreciation*
by Joyce C. Mills, Ph.D., and Richard J. Crowley, Ph.D.
*This Is Me and My Single Parent: A Discovery Workbook for
Children and Single Parents*
by Marla D. Evans
*This Is Me and My Two Families: An Awareness Scrapbook/Journal
for Children Living in Stepfamilies*
by Marla D. Evans